A Simple Guide to Self-Publishing

A time and money-saving handbook to printing,
distributing and promoting your own book.

Second Edition

A WISE OWL BOOK

A Simple Guide to Self-Publishing
Copyright © 1994, 1996 by Mark Ortman
All rights reserved

First Printing: 1994
Second Printing: 1994
Third Printing: Second Edition 1996

ISBN 0-9634699-5-9

Library of Congress Catalog Card Number: 95-62025

Manufactured in the United States of America by Gilliland Printing, Arkansas City KS

WISE OWL BOOKS • Box 621 • Kirkland WA 98083 • USA • (206) 822-9699

Publisher's Cataloging in Publication
(Prepared by Quality Books Inc.)

Ortman, Mark.
    A simple guide to self-publishing: a time and money-saving
handbook to printing, distributing and promoting your own book / by
Mark Ortman. -- 2nd ed.
    p. cm.
    Includes index.
    ISBN 0-9634699-5-9

    1. Self-publishing--Handbooks, manuals, etc. I. Title.
Z285.5.O78 1996   070.5'93
                                        QBI95-20636

This book is not intended as a substitute for legal, accounting
or other professional services. If expert assistance is required,
the services of a competent professional should be sought.

Acknowledgments

A special thanks to the many people who helped make this book possible: Kathleen Kazinski, Rob Ortman and Paul Ortman for their encouragement, Brian Templeton for his savvy recommendations, Herman Liebelt for his tireless reviewing and coaching, Koji Biose for his last minute proofing, John Whaley and APPLE Computer for their help in understanding the World Wide Web, to the students who asked the difficult questions, and of course, the members of the "Big 10" for sharing their expertise and support.

Dedicated to those who are pursuing their dreams.

Contents

Introduction

What do Walt Whitman, William Blake, Benjamin Franklin, Gertrude Stein, D.H. Lawrence, James Joyce and Mark Twain all have in common? They once self-published. Throughout history it has been difficult to find a commercial publisher to finance and distribute your book, and today it is no different. All is not lost. Self-publishing has become one of the fastest growing segments in the publishing industry and is now more feasible because of the computer. With a computer, desk top software (such as Pagemaker/Corel-Ventura/Quark X Press) and a laser printer, anyone can publish a book based on expertise, inspiration or a story.

You may have heard success stories of people who self-published and sold tens of thousands of copies. That does happen. However, publishing is a risky business if you are not careful. The fact remains that out of every ten books published, three earn a profit, four break even and the rest lose money. With those odds it is only sensible to approach this venture wisely.

No one can predict the commercial success of a book. The only way to find out is to give your idea the best possible chance to succeed with the least risk. To write a book is an art, to self-publish it is a business. This is often overlooked until you are stuck with a garage full of unsold books. Your financial risk can be off-set significantly by determining if there is a market for your book. Share your manuscript with members of your target audience, and ask them for an honest assessment. If you are still enthusiastic, print a small quantity and promote your book locally to see how it sells beyond your friends and family. If it sells, print more; if it doesn't, you are not out a fortune. This is called **test marketing**. Other advantages of testing the water before taking the plunge are making intelligent decisions based on facts, not emotions, keeping your day job until your book proves successful, promoting the book in your free time and learning the best way to sell your book as you find your way around the world of publishing.

It is **not** the purpose of this book to be a comprehensive guide to book publishing. That is left to others. The **purpose** of this book is to outline the steps in the self-publishing process in a clear and concise manner. This will answer your initial inquiries: *What do I do first? How do I reduce my risk?* and *Whom do I contact for additional information?* Studying this book will help you to ask informed questions and to better understand the more comprehensive literature written on this subject. Filled with check-lists, references, worksheets and money saving ideas, this guide is designed for the cost conscious self-publisher. Whether you print hundreds or thousands of copies and market them locally or nationally, this book can save you time and money.

The book is organized into five chapters: Getting Started, Printing, Announcing Your Book, Distribution and Creating a Demand. There are two indexes at the back of the book: Subject and Organizations. Each chapter contains tips and references to guide you through the publishing process. This edition also includes information on using the Internet's World Wide Web to distribute and promote your book.

Reading this book is a beginning, not an ending. You are urged to add depth to the ideas on the following pages before you make your final decisions. Self-publishing is not a get-rich-quick scheme and requires hard work and perseverance. I now understand why so many people in this industry have courteously uttered these parting words, similar to those often heard in a gambling casino's token window...
"Good Luck!"

Mark Ortman

Five Reasons to Self-Publish

1. Time. Most commercial publishers work on an 18 month production cycle. Do you want to wait that long to get into print? On your own, it can take 2-6 months after completing the manuscript, depending on the book's marketing plan.

2. Control. If you like the final say on the direction of your projects, then self-publishing will give you this freedom. While other people's experience and advice may be beneficial, why give a third party, whose interests and intentions may be different from your own, the final say? Too many cooks can spoil the stew.

3. Ownership. A commercial publisher would own certain rights to your book, which prevents you from printing copies when he loses interest, allowing him to place your title out of print . . . unless of course you *purchase* those rights back. A self-publisher may sell all, none or a portion of the rights to the book at any time.

4. Make Money. Why accept a 5 to 15% royalty when you can have a 40-400% *(or more)* margin? Sure, a large publisher may have the distribution and will finance the project, but guess who does all the promoting anyway? If your self-published book proves successful, then you can pursue a larger publisher and negotiate from a position of strength.

5. To Be In Print. Not everyone publishes to make money. There are several other reasons, such as: seeing your name in print, leaving a legacy to your family or sharing what you have learned with others. Whatever your motive, a book is a personal expression that can open new possibilities and opportunities. A book takes on a life of its own and you can become a part of that exciting life.

The Three Most Important Questions

Before you decide to publish your own book, know your motivation. Take time to carefully reflect on these three questions, as the answers will help you make some decisions during the publishing process.

1. WHY do you want to publish a book?

2. WHO will buy your book?

3. WHAT makes your book unique?

"The secret to writing a best seller is simply having a good book for which there is a need, at the right price, offered to the right market."

1. Getting Started

Learning About the Industry

❏ There are several sources of information to help you learn about the industry. Before you embark on any major project, it only makes sense to familiarize yourself with the lay of the land. Contact the following organizations and publications to request membership information and magazine samples.

American Booksellers Association (ABA)
828 S Broadway
Tarrytown NY 10591
(800) 637-0037

Also request a list of the regional booksellers associations and a sample of the *American Bookseller* magazine.

COSMEP
Box 703
San Francisco CA 94101
(415) 981-7829

PMA
2401 Pacific Coast Hwy #102-A
Hermosa Beach CA 90254
(310) 372-2732

These two associations provide co-op membership services to independent publishers.

Publishers Weekly
Box 6457
Torrance CA 90504
(800) 278-2991

Small Press Magazine
121 E Front St 4th Fl
Traverse City MI 49684
(616) 933-0445

Request sample copies of the industry's trade journals.

❑ **Visit Local Bookstores.** Tell bookstore owners or store managers you are publishing a book and would like their advice. You may want to call in advance to set up a convenient time to meet. After the meeting, send a thank-you note. When your book is released they may be more inclined to carry your title, especially if you used their ideas.

❑ **Public Libraries** have a wealth of free information. Visit the reference desk and become familiar with the following publications and any others they recommend for the self-publisher.

Literary Market Place
A valuable resource listing agents, associations, book clubs, reviewers, news services, radio and TV stations.

Books in Print & Forthcoming Books
Lists over 1 million titles currently in print in the United States. Also includes the authors' and publishers' names.

❑ **Read Books.** Benefit from other people's experiences by reading their books on self-publishing. I find the following publications to be worthwhile and refer to them often. *These books can be ordered directly through the mail by using the order form on page 60.*

The Self-Publishing Manual	Complete Guide to Self-Publishing
By Dan Poynter	By Tom & Marilyn Ross
ISBN 1-56860-003-8 / $19.95	ISBN 0-89879-646-6 / $18.99

Two very comprehensive books on self-publishing, including what you need to know to write, print and sell your own book.

1001 Ways to Market Your Book
By John Kremer / ISBN 0-912411-42-2 / $19.95

The most complete handbook on book marketing with ideas, tips and suggestions for marketing your own book.

Book Publishing Resource Guide
By Marie Kiefer / ISBN 0-912411-46-5 / $34.95

This directory includes the names, addresses, phone numbers, and key contacts for 1000's of book marketing channels and publicity outlets.

❏ **Online Services & The Internet.** Connect electronically to people with similar interests. Various discussion groups *(newsgroups)* and research archives are accessible to anyone with a computer, modem and online service provider. By doing a search on words such as *books,* a subscriber can browse, converse or post a question to others who may be of help. Below are three commercial online service providers.

America Online	(800) 827-6364
CompuServe	(800) 848-8199
Prodigy	(800) 776-3449

Business Matters

All too often we forget that writing is an art and publishing is a business. For practical, tax and legal reasons it is important to establish a business structure in which your publishing venture can thrive.

❏ Think of a few **names** and **logos** with which to identify your publishing business. Avoid appearing too small by using your own name. Invent a name that is simple, easy to remember, descriptive and that will not limit future publications. Once you have narrowed your choices, check the following resources in the library to avoid name duplication with another publisher.

Small Press Record of Books in Print
Directory of US Publishers
Books in Print

❏ Plan a **budget** for publishing your book. Decisions between what you *want* and what you can *afford* will be easier with a budget. Expect to spend anywhere from $500 to $25,000 depending on the type of book, marketing plan and quantity printed. The three major areas of expense will be:

Book Preparation / Printing / Promotion

> *Tip:* A general guideline for planning the promotional budget is 30-50% of the cost of your first printing.

❏ Apply for a **business license** with your state and local governments. Before you apply, decide on a type of business structure: *Sole Proprietorship*, *Partnership*, or *Corporation*. Most first time publishers choose *Sole Proprietorship* because it is the easiest to form. Talk to a banker, lawyer or the Small Business Administration for advice on starting a business.

Small Business Administration (SBA)
409 3rd St SW
Washington DC 20416
(800) 827-5722 (Answer Desk)

❏ Rent a **Box** from the Post Office for a mailing address to protect your privacy. Request information on bulk mailing permits as well as postal rates. Postage will be a major expense, so know your options to manage mailing costs.

❏ Further professionalize your business image with **printed stationery**. Print letterheads, envelopes, business cards and shipping labels with your name, address and logo. You want to project an image which will instill confidence in people who may want to do business with you. Single title author-publishers must overcome the stigma of being perceived as unprofessional.

Trade Registrations

❑ The *International Standard Book Number* **(ISBN)** is the ten digit number on the back of every book. The numbers identify the publisher and book title. The industry uses this number to order, price and keep track of inventory. Most wholesalers and bookstores are reluctant to stock a book that does not have this number clearly printed on the back cover. The numbers are free through R.R. Bowker. However, there is a handling fee of $165 for the minimum 10 set of numbers. They will arrive on a computer printout sheet reserved for your selection. The remaining nine numbers can be used for your revised editions and future publications.

• After you select a number from the computer printout sheet, activate by completing the **Advance Book Information** form **(ABI)** included with your ISBN order. By submitting an ABI form, your book will be listed in *Books in Print* at no charge. Call R.R. Bowker and request a publisher's information package on how to apply for an ISBN number.

R.R. Bowker (ISBN Agency)
121 Chanlon Rd
New Providence NJ 07974
(908) 665-6770

❑ Set a **publication date** far enough in the future to give you time to print, submit for review, announce your book and generate advance sales. Your publication date is not the date your book comes back from the printer. The publication date is when you are releasing your book for sale to the public. The best publication date for the self-publisher is the first quarter of the year because this allows your copyright date to live a full year and still be new. The two major buying seasons for the publishing industry are Spring and Fall.

❑ **Copyright** protection lasts your life plus 50 years. This is done by using the copyright symbol with the year and your name (Copyright © 1996 by Mark Ortman) and including it on the copyright page of your manuscript. Also, when your manuscript is complete, send yourself a *notarized* copy by *registered mail* and place unopened in storage. This is evidence of a specific date within the copyright year. Finally, when you get your books back from the printer, apply in writing with the copyright office in Washington, DC. *Order in advance the circulars on Copyright and form TX which is package #109. They are free of charge.* Call (202) 707-9100

Registrar of Copyrights
Library of Congress
Washington DC 20559

❑ If you plan to make sales to the library market, apply for a **Library of Congress (LC) Pre-Assigned Card Catalog Number**. Print this number on the copyright page of your book. There is no charge for this number and it can be ordered for any book over 50 pages *(with a few exceptions)*. Request the CIP and PCN publishers manual and forms.

Library of Congress
Cataloging in Publication Division
Washington DC 20540
(202) 707-9797

❑ **Barcodes** (Bookland EAN) are those vertical lines on the back of books. This enables a price scanner to identify the title, ISBN number and price. The cost is about $30 and you need the ISBN number before you can order one. Bookland EAN has become a requirement by most of the book trade.

Data Index, Inc.	**Fotel-GGX Associates, Inc.**
Box 500	6 Grace Avenue
Kirkland WA 98083	Great Neck NY 11021
(800) 426-2183/(206) 885-9081	(516) 487-6370

Preparing the Manuscript

❑ If you use other people's words (not ideas) in your book, get **permission**. Send a request to the publisher by certified mail stating *what you want to quote, how you will use it* and *where you will give credit*. Normally you will get permission without cost. Copying and selling words of another author without written permission is called plagiarism and is illegal. Consult a copyright attorney for specifics.

❑ **Copy Editing.** An editor can clarify and strengthen what you want to say and how you say it. Contact a local newspaper or magazine to see if an editor or writer is willing to do it or recommend a colleague. Another option is to find an English teacher or graduate student from a local college who would love to receive acknowledgment in your book in exchange for assistance.

> *Tip:* In editing: review slowly, question everything and ask yourself, "Are the statements I am making true and verifiable?"

❑ Ask five eagle-eyed friends to **proofread** your manuscript for consistency, spelling, usage and punctuation. Do not rely on your computer's spell checker since it doesn't know whether you want to use, for example: "to", "too" or "two". It is not uncommon to rewrite your manuscript a dozen times before it is ready to print . . . so be patient. Changes become costly after the manuscript goes to the printer. Include those people who help, in the book's acknowledgments.

> *Tip:* Realize how editing and proofreading influence the quality of your book. Seek competent help in these areas to reduce post-printing regrets.

❏ **Typesetting & Layout.** This has to do with the placement of your illustrations, graphs, pictures and text. In other words, how the inside of your book will look. Research books in bookstores and libraries to use as models for your own layout. A professional typesetter's fee can range from $4-10 per page. Thus it may be cost-effective to purchase a computer, software and even a printer to do it yourself. Today's laser printers can produce clear camera-ready 600 DPI (dots per inch) text output at a reasonable price. The goal of the layout is to make your book easy to read and use. Ask yourself if the text, layout and illustrations communicate a consistent message throughout your book.

• **Page Layout Margins.** The layout margin is the space between the edge of the paper and where the text starts. That compensates for trimming during the printing process. Save money by selecting a standard size for your book: 5.5 x 8.5, 6 x 9 or 8.5 x 11. Typically a 1/2" to 1.5" margin is adequate, depending on the design, size of paper and type of binding you use. For example: this book uses a 5/8" margin.

• **Typeface & Font.** Most books use a Serif typeface for the *main body* of the text instead of Sans Serif type because it is easier to read and looks more professional. See the sample below. Handwritten copy or calligraphy may be suitable for certain publications, such as poetry or children's books. However, too much handwritten copy is hard to read and may detract from the flavor and intention of your book.

Serif   Sans Serif

• **Illustrations.** Illustrations can range from charts, photographs and artwork to anything that is not typeset. In planning the layout, leave enough space for the illustrations and either scan them in with a computer or paste them in by hand. Consult a graphic artist.

The Cover Design

The goal of the cover design is to get people's attention. Books are often sold on the merits of the cover alone; thus the cover should capture the essence of your book. It is worth the investment to hire a **graphic artist** with *book design experiencce*. Expect to pay $350 for a basic one color design to over $2,000 for a full color camera-ready design.

❑ People's first impressions come from the title of your book. Keep your **book title** brief, vivid and descriptive. The title should be legible from 10 feet so people strolling though the bookstore can read it at a glance. The **subtitle** gives you an added sales message, describing your book in greater detail. Once you have narrowed possible book titles, check *Books in Print* and *Forthcoming Books* for a title clearance.

❑ If you think the book's **spine** is unimportant in the design, consider how many books in a bookstore are faced out that way. Include on the spine the title of the book, author's and publisher's names and logo.

❑ The **back cover** should convince the potential book buyers they are making the right decision by purchasing your book. Make it easy, interesting and informative for the browser to review. The back cover might include:

- Book's description and benefits to the reader
- Reviews, Endorsements or Testimonials
- Author's bio and picture
- ISBN, Bar Code, Price and Subject Category

❑ The easiest way to get **testimonials** or **endorsements** is to ask for them. Ask experts or celebrities in your field to review your manuscript and submit their impressions. Get permission in writing to print their comments on your book cover.

"Whenever I am asked what kind writing is the most lucrative . . . I have to say, ransom notes!"

H.N. Swanson

2. Printing

Book Manufacturers

Get bids from a *Book Manufacturer* instead of a local printer. Book manufacturers have the equipment to print and bind books themselves, instead of sending out the work and marking up the price. If your book is more than 60 pages and you are printing over 100 copies, chances are the prices will be lower through a book manufacturer.

❏ Cheapest isn't always best. Consider **quality, service,** and **support.** If a problem arises - and printing is fertile ground for problems - whose side will your printer be on, yours or his? Paying a little more for peace of mind is often worth it. Request samples, and check references before you decide.

❏ Request **blueline proofs** and **matchprint** from your printer before your book goes to final press. This means you'll see and approve what the text and cover color will look like before it is printed. Check for typographical errors or pages missing or out of sequence. There may be a charge for this service, but it is comforting to have the chance to make last minute changes.

❏ Most printers will print about 10% too many or too few books. These are called **over-** or **under-runs.** Ask what the over-runs will cost. They usually cost less, thus lowering the overall cost per copy of your book. Reprints are usually less expensive from the same printer because of reduced setup costs. Still, get other quotes to keep everyone honest.

❑ It's more economical to print in **even signatures.** This means the number of pages a printing press can print at one time. Most book manufacturers use a 16 or 32 page signature *(depending on the book size).* Divide the pages of your book into 16 or 32 and you will know how many signatures the printer will use. If your book is a page or two over an even signature, reduce the printing cost by editing out a page or two.

❑   **Retail Price.** Search bookstores for comparable books to use as price models. A common mistake for self-publishers is to price their book either too high or too low. Printing costs do affect the retail price of the book. Don't expect your first printing to be very profitable, particularly when printing a small quantity. Reprints are more profitable because of reduced printing costs, assuming you don't make many changes to the book. Also keep in mind the percentage you will give away for distribution. *(See page 33.)*

Preparing a Printing Estimate

To prepare a price quote from a book manufacturer, you will need to know:

- Quantity
- Total page count
- Type of paper (text and cover)
- How many colors on the cover and cover coating
- Type of binding
- Size of the book
- Number of pictures (Black and white or color)
- Packaging and shipping costs

❑ **Quantity.** How many books should you order? The more you print, the less each costs. Strike a balance between printing enough copies to keep your unit cost down and too many copies where you're stuck with a garage full of unsold books. Typically, small publishers will order between 500 and 3500 books in the first printing. The only time to order more is if most are pre-sold. You can always re-order when your inventory gets low. Reprints generally cost less if there are not many changes made. Changes require the cost of new printing plates. Plan on 4 to 5 weeks for delivery.

❑ **Page Count.** To figure the total page count in your book, include the *front* and the *back* matter. The front matter is all the pages before the main text such as: *Title Pages, Copyright Page, Acknowledgments, Preface, Foreword, Introduction, Table of Contents, Dedication.* The back matter includes all pages in a book after the main text: *Afterword, Appendix, Bibliography, Glossary, Index, etc...*

❑ **Paper.** Unless you are doing an art or specialty book, most printers will suggest a 50, 60, or 70 lb. white offset. (Recycled paper is more expensive.) The higher the weight, the heavier and less opaque the paper. The thickness (bulk) of the paper is measured by PPI (pages per inch). Ask the printer for this number to determine the width of the book's spine. The lower the PPI, the bulkier the paper, thus the thicker the book.

> *Tip:* One of your greatest expenses will be postage and shipping. The paper you select will influence this expense. Heavier paper costs more to ship.

❑ **Cover Paper.** Will the book be softcover or hardcover? Because of lower production costs, most books are now softcover. The standard paper for softcover is a 10 or 12 point C1S (coated one side) cover stock. Hardcover books will use a dust jacket, and 80 or 100 lb enamel paper is most common. Order five to ten percent extra book covers or dust jackets as they are useful for various promotional purposes.

❏ **Cover Coating.** This is what protects the book cover and enhances the color. There are various kinds available, such as lay flat plastic lamination, UV, matted or aqueous coating. Ask the printers what type they use and the advantages of each. Also ask them to send you samples.

❏ **Binding.** This is what holds the book together. Some common types are: Perfect Bound (softcover), Otabind (lays open), Case Bound (hardcover), Spiral or Saddle Stitched (stapled). How the book will be used will influence the type of binding. The most popular and prudent is Perfect Bound.

> *Tip:* Bookstores frown upon Spiral and Saddle Stitched because you can't read them when faced spine out on the shelf.

❏ **Book Size.** The conventional and common 5.5 x 8.5 is suitable for both hard and softcover, and is one of the most economical to print. Other standard sizes include 6 x 9 and 8.5 x 11. The further you get away from the standard, the more expensive it is to produce.

❏ **Pictures.** Color photos can be beautiful, although the cost may be prohibitive because of color separation and extra print run fees. B&W photos are more practical and affordable. All B&W photographs require halftones. The process of creating a halftone converts the picture into dots of various sizes and shades of gray. The more dots per inch, the clearer the picture. Most halftones for books are produced at 120-133 dots per inch. Consult your graphic artist for details.

❏ **Packaging.** Ask your printer the most economical way to ship your books. Plan for storage by asking the printer the size and weight of the cartons. A packaging option to consider is shrink wrapping. This is a clear plastic wrap used to protect the books and should be considered if you intend to store your books in a garage or unheated area.

List of Book Manufacturers

These printers specialize in the manufacturing of books. For additional listings, see the *Literary Market Place* in a library. Get all estimates **in writing** before you make a decision.

BookCrafters
613 E Industrial Dr
Chelsea MI 48118
(313) 475-9145
Fax (313) 475-7337

McNaughton & Gunn
960 Woodland Dr
Saline MI 48176
(313) 429-5411
Fax (313) 429-4033

Braun-Brumfield
100 N Staebler Rd
Ann Arbor MI 48106
(313) 662-3291
Fax (313) 662-1667

Malloy Lithographing
5411 Jackson Rd
Ann Arbor MI 48103
(313) 665-6113
Fax (313) 665-2326

Edwards Brothers
2500 S State St
Ann Arbor MI 48106
(313) 769-1000
Fax (313) 769-0350

Gilliland Printing
215 N Summit
Arkansas City KS 67005
(316) 442-8500
Fax (316) 442-8504

Thomson-Shore
7300 W Joy Rd
Dexter MI 48130
(313) 426-3939
Fax (313) 426-6216

Data Reproductions
1480 N Rochester Rd
Rochester Hills MI 48307
(810) 652-7600
Fax (810) 652-7605

Ultra Short-Run Book Printers (*100 to 1000 copies*)

C & M Press
4825 Nome St
Denver CO 80239
(303) 375-9922
Fax (303) 375-8699

Morgan Printing
900 Old Koenig Ln #135
Austin TX 78756
(512) 459-5194
Fax (512) 451-0755

Printing Estimate Worksheet

Quantity: _____ Trim Size: _____ x _____ Pages: _____

Photos/Halftones: _____ ❏ Color ❏ B & W ❏ Bleeds

Paper

❏ 50 lb Book   ❏ Other: _____

❏ 60 lb Book   ❏ Color: _____

The PPI (pages per inch) of paper _____

Text Ink color: ❏ Black   ❏ Other: _____

Cover

❏ 10 pt. C1S   ❏ 80 lb Enamel (Hardcover)

❏ 12 Pt. C1S   ❏ Other: _____

Cover Colors / Coating

Cover color Black + _____ Colors

Bleeds   Yes   No

Cover Coating: ❏ Film Lamination ❏ Matte ❏ Other: _____

Quantity of extra covers: _____

Binding

❏ Perfect (Soft)   ❏ Case (Hard)   ❏ Staple (Saddle)   ❏ _____

Copy & Cover to be furnished:

❏ Text camera-ready ❏ Cover Film Negatives ❏ Computer Disk

Cost per book of over-runs: _____

Cost per extra 1000 books ordered: _____

Shipping Costs & Instructions:

Printing Estimate Worksheet

Quantity: _____ Trim Size: _____ x _____ Pages: _____

Photos/Halftones: _____ ❏ Color ❏ B & W ❏ Bleeds

Paper

    ❏ 50 lb Book   ❏ Other: _____

    ❏ 60 lb Book   ❏ Color: _____

    The PPI (pages per inch) of paper _____

    Text Ink color: ❏ Black   ❏ Other: _____

Cover

    ❏ 10 pt. C1S   ❏ 80 lb Enamel (Hardcover)

    ❏ 12 Pt. C1S   ❏ Other: _____

Cover Colors / Coating

    Cover color Black + _____ Colors

    Bleeds   Yes   No

Cover Coating: ❏ Film Lamination ❏ Matte ❏ Other: _____

    Quantity of extra covers: _____

Binding

❏ Perfect (Soft) ❏ Case (Hard) ❏ Staple (Saddle) ❏ _____

Copy & Cover to be furnished:

❏ Text camera-ready ❏ Cover Film Negatives ❏ Computer Disk

Cost per book of over-runs: _____

Cost per extra 1000 books ordered: _____

Shipping Costs & Instructions:

*"Publishing is a very mysterious business.
It is hard to predict what kind of sale
or reception a book will have."*

Thomas Wolfe

3. Announcing Your Book

Letting the Industry Know

❏ Let the book trade know you have published a book. Orders can come most unexpectedly by having your title listed in several directories. Most of these listings are free. Write or phone to request an application.

International Standard Book Numbering Agency (ISBN)
When you submit your **ABI** (Advanced Book Information) form with your publication date and ISBN number, you will automatically be listed in *Books in Print*.

Library of Congress Catalog Card Number.
When you request an LC number, your book will be listed in a catalog enabling libraries to locate your book more easily.

Cumulative Book Index & Vertical File Index
H.W. Wilson Co
950 University Ave
Bronx NY 10452
(718) 588-8400

Small Press Record of Books in Print &
International Directory of Little Magazines and Small Presses.
Dustbooks
Box 100
Paradise CA 95967
(916) 877-6110

ABA Book Buyers Handbook
American Booksellers Assn
828 S Broadway
Tarrytown NY 10591
(800) 637-0037

Any Book
The Library Corporation
Research Park
Inwood WV 25428
(800) 624-0559

Pre-Publication Reviews

In addition to yourself, who else thinks your book is great? Pre-publication reviews are directed at the trade (libraries, wholesalers and bookstores) **before** the publication date and the release of your book. This helps the trade evaluate new titles and influences its purchasing decisions.

❑ **Trade Reviews.** At least 90 days *before* your publication date, send to the major review magazines listed below: galleys (NOT a book), a photocopy of your ABI form, sample of the cover art (if possible), and a cover letter describing *why* you wrote the book and *how* it is unique. Send by first class mail. There is no guarantee your book will be reviewed. However, one favorable review could generate substantial advance sales. In addition, any reviews you receive can be used on your promotional literature and printed on the back cover of reprinted books. It is worth a phone call to inquire about the full name (with correct spelling) of the person to whom to submit a review package and his submission requirements. See *Literary Market Place* for more reviewers.

Booklist
American Library Assn
50 E Huron St
Chicago IL 60611
(312) 944-6780

Chicago Tribune Books
435 N Michigan Ave
Chicago Il 60611
(312) 222-3232

Kirkus Reviews
200 Park Ave S
New York NY 10003
(212) 777-4554

Library Journal
249 W 17th St
New York NY 10011
(212) 645-0067

L.A. Times Book Review Times Mirror Square Los Angeles CA 90053 (213) 237-5000	**N.Y. Times Review of Books** 250 W 57th St New York NY 10107 (212) 757-8070
N.Y. Times Book Review 229 W 43rd St, 8th Fl New York NY 10036 (212) 556-1942	**Publishers Weekly** 249 W 17th St New York NY 10011 (212) 645-0067
San Francisco Chronicle Book Review 275 5th St San Francisco CA 94103 (415) 777-7042	**Small Press** 121 E Front St 4th Fl Traverse City MI 49684 (616) 933-0445
San Francisco Review of Books 126 S Park San Francisco CA 94107 (415) 543-7372	**Bloomsbury Review** 1762 Emerson St Denver CO 80218 (303) 863-0406

• **Galleys.** A galley is not a finished book, but a representation of the finished book. Instead of paying to have galley proofs printed and bound, consider making copies of your camera-ready manuscript you furnished the printer.

• **News Release.** The best news releases are those which read like a well-written newspaper article. Your goal is to make the release interesting and informative. On one page (double-spaced) answer: the *Who, What, Why, When* and *Where* . . . about your book, not in a self-serving manner, but factually. Stay away from hype, and focus on what problem your book addresses and its value. Also, include the book's trade specification such as: author information, publication date, number of pages, size, price, binding, ISBN number and an optional picture of the cover.

> *"The critic is the only independent source of information, The rest is advertising."*
> Pauline Kael

Post-Publication Reviews

Post-publication reviews are intended to reach the purchaser of your book. It is very expensive and inefficient to send review copies to every book reviewer. Target those from whom you have the best chance of getting a review.

❏ **Newspapers.** Most newspaper book reviewers receive more solicitations daily than they can review in a month. Review space is at a premium. Nevertheless, any mention of your book will help sales. If your book has a general appeal, at least 45 days before your release date, mail a news release and book request postcard to the many major newspapers in the country. Target the appropriate editor. Rent a mailing list from one of the mailing list managers on page 51-52. Local newspapers and magazines are your best bets to get a book review or an article. Because you are local news, they will be more inclined to give you preference over others.

❏ **Magazine Reviews.** Target people who will purchase and read your book. Find out what magazines *they* read and send a copy of your book, a press release and cover letter to those magazines' book review editors. See the *Book Publishing Resource Guide* by *Marie Kiefer,* or a copy of *Magazines for Libraries* in the public library for listings of specialty magazines.

❏ **Free-Lance Reviewers.** Rent a mailing list of free-lance book reviewers around the country (see page 51). Send a news release, copy of your ABI form, and a book request return postcard 45 days before the book is released.

❏ **Experts in the Field.** Send a review copy to authorities or experts on the subject of your book asking for their endorsements. This is a wonderful way to get influential people talking about your book. See *Who's Who in America* at the local library for their names and addresses.

❏ **Newsletter Reviews.** The number of newsletters now published has boomed during the past decade, accounting for nearly one-third of all publications. This has resulted in more opportunities to get your book reviewed or mentioned for your market audience. See the *Oxbridge Directory of Newsletters* in the local library.

• **Review Copies.** Giving books away can become an expensive proposition, particularly when you include the cost of postage. A simple rule is to budget *at least* 10% of the books from your first printing as review copies and give them to the people who can *do you the most good*. Be flexible in giving away review copies as they can be an extremely good investment. Of course, with your second printing, you can afford to be more liberal in your giveaways. Stamp REVIEW COPY, NOT FOR SALE on any copy you give away to discourage people from selling or returning that book to wholesalers for a refund. Keep good records of giveaways as they are a tax-deductible business expense.

Book Review Tips

Choose only those reviewers most suitable to the subject of your book.

Follow up immediately with anyone who requests a review copy of your book.

Don't be surprised if you don't get an overwhelming response from all the reviewers.

"There are books of which the backs and covers are by far the best parts."
Charles Dickens

*"Literature is like any other trade;
you will never sell anything unless
you go to the right shop."*

George Bernard Shaw

4. Distribution

Distribution Channels

How are people going to find your book if they decide to buy it? Reviews, publicity and promotion are worthless unless your book is easily available to the reader. At least 2-4 months before the release date, decide on how you will distribute your book; whether through conventional, alternative or a combination of both channels of distribution.

❏ **Consignments.** This means you don't get paid until after your book is sold. This is a standard practice in the publishing industry, especially in the conventional channels of distribution. All books are sold on a consignment basis unless terms are negotiated differently. Also, it is common practice to return all unsold books to you when the demand ceases.

❏ **Marketing Plan.** Most channels of distribution want to know how *you* are going to create a demand for your book if they stock it. That's right, the self-publisher is responsible for creating the demand. Before you approach the conventional channels of distribution, have a 12 month step-by-step marketing plan *(See page 41)* for your book which answers:

- **WHO** is your target audience?

- **HOW** will you reach them? **WHAT** will you do?

- **WHEN** will each step of the plan be implemented?

Conventional Channels of Distribution

❑ **Bookstores.** There are many kinds of bookstores: General, Used, College, Religious to list a few. Independently owned bookstores make up nearly half of all the bookstores in the United States. Half of those (and growing) are chains such as Barnes & Noble, Borders and Crown. The standard bookstore discount is 40% off the list price. Bookstores purchase a majority of their books through wholesalers. Most bookstores prefer buying books through a wholesaler or distributor because they carry numerous titles, simplifying their ordering procedure. *The American Book Trade Directory* in the library has bookstore listings.

❑ **Chain Bookstores.** Growing segments in the industry are the chains and superstores. Their inventories are tightly controlled with short shelf life for slow-moving books. Recognize the risk of selling to the chains. They may order your entire stock and pay you 90 days later, leaving you to finance the next printing. Then, all of a sudden, they return the unsold books asking for a refund. A more cautious approach would be to coordinate purchases and promotional effort with local or regional chain buyers. This way the sales of one area finance the expansion into another. Why risk putting all your books in one basket?

❑ **Wholesalers.** Wholesalers stock, pick, pack, ship and collect, then pay you 90 days later on orders received for your book. For this service, they want a 55% discount off the list price. Most are *"Demand Wholesalers"* meaning they fulfill orders for your book based on the demand that *you* create. There are hundreds of book wholesalers in the country, some national, some regional and many specializing in niche markets. To find their specialties, consult the *Book Publishing Resource Guide* by *Marie Kiefer* or *Literary Market Place* in the library.

INGRAM Book Company and **Baker & Taylor Books** are the nation's largest general book wholesalers with branches throughout the United States. Contact each of them and ask how to start a vendor account.

Baker & Taylor Books
652 E Main St
Bridgewater NJ 08807
(908) 218-3803

INGRAM Book Company
One Ingram Blvd
LaVergne TN 37086
(615) 793-5000 Ext 7584

Is your book of mainly local or regional interest? Ask local booksellers which regional wholesaler(s) they order through. Contact that wholesaler, tell him your marketing plans, and establish a vendor account.

❏ **Distributors.** Distributors differ from wholesalers in that they sell your book through commissioned sales reps and a catalog. Depending on your marketing plan and the nature of your book, a distributor will introduce your title to wholesalers and bookstores, thus freeing you to concentrate on promotion. Their fee is 55% to 68% off the list price. Some may require an exclusive arrangement. Before signing an exclusive agreement, clarify **what** is meant by "exclusive". Do not limit your book to an exclusive arrangement, preventing you from selling to markets which the distributor doesn't sell to. Contact distributors 60-180 days before your book is released to allow them enough time to go through their selection committees. Listed next are the various types of distributors. See the *Literary Market Place* or the *Book Publishing Resource Guide* for additional listings.

• **Mass Market Distributors.** If your book fits their format they will place your title in non-bookstore locations such as supermarkets, airports, and newsstands. Their fee: 55% off list. Require all returns in resalable condition. Mass Market distributors traditionally have a high return rate and a short shelf life. If a book doesn't sell *fast*, it is replaced.

• **Specialty Distributors.** When your book is targeted toward a specific niche or subject area (Outdoor, Health, Ethnic, etc.), specialty distributors can help you reach that reader. Their fees vary between 55% to 68% off list.

• **Library Distributors.** They specialize in selling books to libraries. Contact the two distributors listed below and ask for a vendor application. Both work on consignment and want a 55% discount and pay 90 days after each book is sold.

Quality Books
1003 W Pines Rd
Oregon IL 61061
(815) 732-4450

Unique Books
4230 Grove Ave
Gurnee IL 60031
(847) 623-9171

• **National General Distributors.** If your book is of general interest and you plan to promote your title nationally, contract a general titled national distributor to carry your book. A distributor will get your book to the major regional and national book wholesalers and perhaps present your title to major independent and chain bookstores. A distributor will coordinate your promotional efforts with his national sales rep network. Distributors want a 65-68% discount off list. Below are six national distributors you can request information from on their title acquisition procedure. Most will want an exclusive right to sell in the book trade (bookstores and libraries). That leaves you to sell through alternative channels. Have a detailed marketing plan before approaching these distributors.

Atrium Publishers Group
3356 Coffey Lane
Santa Rosa CA 95403
(707) 542-5400

BookWorld Services, Inc.
1933 Whitfield Loop
Sarasota FL 34243
(813) 758-8094

Independent Publishers Group
814 N Franklin St
Chicago IL 60610
(312) 337-0747

Login Publishers Consortium
1436 W Randolph St
Chicago IL 60607
(312) 733-8228

National Book Network
4720 Boston Way
Lanham MD 20706
(301) 459-8696

Publishers Group West
4065 Hollis St
Emeryville CA 94608
(510) 658-3453

Alternative Channels of Distribution

If your book does not have broad, general appeal for conventional channels of distribution, all is not lost. Most books sold in the United States are sold through alternative channels. Books on a specific subject or niche may find alternative channels easiest to secure and most profitable. Consult the *Literary Market Place* or *The Book Publishing Resource Guide* for additional listings of alternative distributors.

❑ **Book Clubs.** Book clubs may be interested in purchasing book club rights or actual copies of your book when printed. While some special interest book clubs will buy books regardless of the publication date, most prefer 6 months notice before the publication date.

❑ **Catalog Houses.** Have you ever received a catalog in the mail that featured books? Thousands of companies in the United States send out catalogs annually, many including books. Send a copy of your book before the publication date to mail order catalog companies that specialize in the subject area of your title. For mail order catalogs that feature books see *Directory of Mail Order Catalogs* by Grey House Publishing at the public library and the *Book Publishing Resource Guide.*

❏ **Gift Representatives.** Over 30% of the population have never been in a bookstore. Having your book displayed in retail outlets such as gift and card shops is a way to reach some of those people. Unlike bookstores, the gift market does not return books. However, the discount is a little higher; generally 50% off list. Gift representatives present your title to buyers at a 10-15% commission. You are then responsible for shipping and invoicing the books they sell.

❏ **Special Sales.** Home improvement centers, drugstores, auto supply dealers, kitchen shops, health food stores are all prospects if your book fits their niche. In other words, approach people or companies who can tie your book into the marketing of their own products. Most of these sales are made on a non-return basis.

❏ **Direct Sales.** Any sales made bypassing a middle man are your most profitable. You keep 100% of the retail price less any expenses and negotiated discounts.

❏ **Fulfillment Services.** These companies offer warehousing and order-processing services (800 numbers & credit card purchases over the phone) for your book. Most want a 35% to 50% discount off list. As you promote your title, make reference to the service's 800 number for ordering 24 hours a day. Shipping and handling costs are paid for by the purchaser. Contact the following about their services.

Twin Peaks Press	**Upper Access**
Box 129	Box 457
Vancouver WA 98666	Hinesburg VT 05461
(360) 694-2462	(802) 482-2988
Thunderbird Fulfillment	**BookMasters, Inc.**
5501 N 7th Ave #116	2541 Ashland Rd
Phoenix AZ 85013	Mansfield OH 44905
(602) 241-6677	(419) 589-5100

❑ **Online Bookstores (Internet).** These are businesses that have a Web Site on the Internet and will list your book in their electronic bookstore for a fee. People around the world can browse a book's contents, read excerpts, and get ordering information from their computer. Watch for special interest bookstores that are emerging on the Web that may closely match your book's market niche. Be cautious about signing *any* exclusive agreement to your book's electronic rights.

Book Stacks Unlimited	**The Bookzone**
200 Public Sq #26-4600	Box 2228
Cleveland OH 44114	Scottsdale, AZ 85252
(216) 861-0467	(602) 481-9737
info@books.com	bookzone@ttx.com

❑ **Subsidiary Rights.** This is when you sell the rights of all or a portion of your book to someone else who will package it in a different form for his market. Some examples include: movie/TV rights, an excerpt for a magazine article, paperback or hardcover rights, electronic rights and foreign rights.

❑ **Remainder Dealers.** Remainder dealers help liquidate overstocks and remaining copies of your out-of-print books. They will purchase unsold books at pennies on the dollar. When all sales sources are exhausted, contact several remainder dealers to see who will give you the best price and terms.

❑ **Donations.** Another way to liquidate unsold books is to donate remaining and damaged books to a worthy cause or non-profit groups and take the tax write-off.

"Writing is the only profession where no one considers you ridiculous if you earn no money."
Jules Renard

"The writing of a best-seller represents only a fraction of the total effort required to create one."

Ted Nicholas

5. Creating a Demand

Developing a Marketing Plan

Marketing your book is generally the most important and demanding aspect of self-publishing. There are over 500 new titles released each week, over one million books in print and the average bookstore stocks only 25,000 titles. This contributes to a very crowded and competitive environment. The trade has just one question: **"Will your book sell?"**

A book is a product, and like any other product requires publicity and promotion. Potential readers must be made **aware** of your book, **how** it differs from similar books on the market and **where** they can purchase it. Proper planning is essential to give your book the best chance of success; in other words. . . develop a marketing plan. When you know where you are going, it is easier to get there.

❑ **A Marketing Plan** answers the questions: *WHO* will buy your book? *HOW* will you reach those people? *WHEN* will you reach those people?

• **WHO?** A technique to help you figure out *Who will buy your book* is to compile a list of organizations, occupations, associations, hobbyists and anyone who will find value in owning your book. List those you want to reach first, second, third, etc. Review the list and see if there is any overlap. This will help you direct your efforts most efficiently and give you insight into HOW to best reach your customer.

• **HOW?** How will you let the reader know about your book and where to purchase copies? The self-publisher actually has **two** categories of customers: *The Trade* and *The Reader*. The Trade consists of bookstores, wholesalers and libraries. The Reader is your target audience or end user. Marketing efforts should be allocated to both, particularly when using conventional channels of distribution. There are six ways to reach people through your promotions: *Mail, Fax, Phone, Computer, The Media* and *In Person,* each having its advantages and disadvantages. Your choice of distribution may help determine the medium by which you will reach your audience. People today are more accessible, yet harder to sell, stressing the importance of a tightly targeted and strong sales message.

Tip: It is not uncommon for a talk show host to receive over 50 solicitations for interviews or publicity each week. In such a crowded arena, a weak message will get little response. Telephone is the most effective way to reach these people.

• **WHEN?** When is the Trade and the Reader in the most favorable buying mood? Does your book have a seasonal twist? Publishers introduce new releases throughout the year with an emphasis on two seasons: Spring and Fall. The industry's largest trade show, the American Booksellers Association convention, occurs annually around the end of May. This is a key time for publishers to show their new titles to the Trade. Readers purchase books throughout the year with an emphasis on the holiday and gift seasons. The nature of your book is also a consideration as the timing may be built into your product and the reader or industry you intend to reach.

"I have no fans. You know what I got? Customers!
Mickey Spillane

Promotional Tool Kit

There is no limit to what you can spend on promotional materials. It becomes a question of budget and what is practical. Below are suggestions for a basic promotional tool kit for the budget minded self-publisher.

- **News Release.** The one page news release answers *Who, What, When,* and *Why* you wrote the book concentrating on what problem and solution your book will address for the reader. This is what is mailed to announce the release of your book to reviewers, bookstores and the media. Keep it simple, informative and interesting.

- **Extra Book Covers.** Extra book covers come in handy as mailers, point of purchase display and can be used as part of your media kit. Many distributors will request extra covers for their sales force to use to sell your title.

- **Media Kit.** This is sent to the media to prepare them for an interview. Include background about the author, details about the book and a list of possible interview questions. Make it informative and straightforward as most interviewers will not read your book.

- **Photos.** Order black and white promo glossies of the front cover of your book and another one of you. Pictures are sometimes requested by reviewers, magazines, newspapers and bookstores to promote signings. Include them in some of your mailings in the hope of having a picture beside a review or article. The following company specializes in quantity discounted glossies.

Ornaal Glossies, Inc.
24 W 25th St
New York NY 10010
(800) 826-6312

- **Reviews, Endorsements & Letters.** Save any reviews, endorsements, testimonials, fan mail and articles written about you or your book. These provide great sales copy for your promotional literature.

- **ABI Form.** Include a completed Advance Book Information form in your mailings to all **pre**-publication reviewers. This gives them pertinent book information, and is helpful in qualifying and writing a review.

- **Book Request Postcard.** Print book request return postcards and include one with your press release when you are not sending a review copy of your book. Those interested in your press release message will respond, thus saving you the expense of mailing books randomly to uninterested people.

- **Brochure, Flyer or Postcard.** A full color flyer is useful, catchy and professional. A helpful hint is to leave some blank space on the front or the back side to photocopy a specific promotional message at a future date. This enables you to adjust your flyer's message and use for many promotional situations. A 4x6 color post card with your cover printed on one side can save on postage and envelope costs. Shop around, as prices vary from printer to printer.

- **Specialty Advertising.** If your budget permits, imprinted bookmarks, pens, T-shirts, buttons, coffee mugs and the like are a fun giveaway and reminder of your book. It is not uncommon to charge people for unique or unusual specialty advertising items. They can also become a part of your product line.

'If you want to persuade people, show the immediate relevance and value of what you're saying in meeting their needs and desires."
Herb Cohen

Ways to Create a Demand

The most consuming facet of self-publishing is to create a demand for your book. Few titles come off the press instant best sellers. Listed below are some of the most useful ways to make people aware of your book. With so many options, self-publishers have the luxury of time to systematically test several promotional strategies to find what works best. What works for one book may not work for another. A more comprehensive collection of ideas can be found in *1001 Ways to Market Your Book* by *John Kremer*.

❏ **Book Signings.** Unless your signing is backed by a great deal of media promotion it is doubtful that people will be lined up waiting for your autograph. However, the signing serves other purposes: it gets your book displayed in the store; you begin building a relationship with the store owner, manager and staff (who become familiar with your title and may recommend it to their customers) and you leave behind signed copies which increase the book's appeal. Most bookstores are receptive to signings, as your presence will help pull customers into their store, resulting in free publicity for them. Send the local media advance notice of your signing; most will list this free.

❏ **More on Libraries.** There are more than 100,000 libraries in the United States ranging from Academic to Public Libraries, and they buy a lot of books. Libraries will purchase your book at the profitable list price and your title becomes a permanent advertisement when sitting on their shelves. Do not overlook local libraries for generating publicity and reviews through signings, workshops and lectures. Many Public Libraries have an events coordinator or "Friends of the Library" groups who organize author and fundraising activities.

❏ **Readings & Lectures**. Local social, civic and business organizations are all looking for speakers. Use your expertise and promote your book. Most groups will let you sell directly to members after the presentation.

❏ **Seminars.** If you enjoy teaching and speaking, find a group, business or organization to sponsor and promote your seminar. This will help offset any costs incurred and provide a built-in endorsement for you and your book.

❏ **Write an Article.** Since you know more about your topic than most people, share your knowledge and promote your book at the same time. There are many newsletters, magazines and newspapers that welcome newsworthy articles.

❏ **Trade Shows & Conventions.** Selling your book at a trade show or convention can be a profitable experience. Assembled in one place is a high concentration of potential buyers. This becomes a great place to make valuable contacts and get exposure to an industry. Use the *Encyclopedia of Associations* in the library to find out what groups are holding meetings or conventions in your vicinity. The *Chamber of Commerce* and the city's *Convention Centers* are also helpful.

❏ **Book Trade Shows.** The primary purpose of a regional or national book trade show is to introduce new titles to the trade. You may display your new book on your own or pay someone else to do so. Bookstore owners who attend will browse and make seasonal buying decisions; this is an ideal opportunity to win shelf space in their stores.

❏ **Book, Art & Street Fairs.** Sponsors promote to the general public or to a niche group of people and thus are a great forum for showing and selling your book direct. Calculate your break-even point before paying for space. Sharing space with another author can reduce costs.

❏ **Fundraisers.** Most groups, schools and organizations are looking for ways to generate revenues. If there is a subject tie-in, donate a percentage of your book sales to their cause in exchange for selling and endorsing your book.

❏ **Premium & Incentive.** Many businesses offer premiums as incentives to their employees and customers. Why shouldn't that premium be your book? See the *Thomas Registry* in the library for a listing of companies and products to find a tie-in.

❏ **Book Awards & Contests.** An award or even being nominated for a book award can be a profitable and satisfying experience, generating free publicity for your book. Submit your title to the various organizations that offer such contests. See the *Literary Market Place* or *Writer's Market* in the library for a listing.

❏ **The Media.** The media (radio, newspapers, television and magazines) is under pressure to fill space or time with news. Make you and your book sound newsworthy and interesting before approaching them. The media is a great way to get free publicity. Locally, you and your book are news and should have an edge to get air time or print space. See *The Directory of Publications and Broadcast Media* in the library. In addition to mail list managers, the following companies sell ways to reach the national media.

Radio-TV Interview Report	**Talk Show Selects**
Bradley Communications Corp.	Broadcast Interview Source
135 E Plumstead Ave	2233 Wisconsin Ave NW
Lansdowne PA 19050	Washington DC 20007
(215) 259-1070	(202) 333-4904
(800) 989-1400	(800) 955-0311

"The oldest books are still only just out to those who have not read them."
Samuel Butler

• **Radio.** If you enjoy talking about your book, you will enjoy radio interviews. There are over 750 radio talk shows in the country looking for interesting guests. Many conduct interviews over the phone, which means you don't have to leave your home. Some will even tape an interview to be aired at a future date. Phone the Program Director or Producer of the station and ask if they do author interviews. Be prepared to explain why your message will be important to their listeners. Make an interview with you sound appealing. Start off by interviewing on smaller stations to practice your message for the larger ones.

Assume the interviewer has not read your book. This is the case more often than not and he will rely on the materials you send him in advance. Your *Media Kit* should include detailed information about the author, the book, and possible interview questions the interviewer could ask. Radio is one of the most accessible forms of publicity. (Phone bookstores prior to your radio interview to insure they have your book in stock. See *The American Book Trade Directory* in the library.)

• **Newspapers.** Perhaps your book solves a lifestyle, business, gardening, travel or cooking problem. Send an article you have written to the appropriate editor, with permission to use all or part of your writing. If your book solves a problem that just hit the headlines, get on the phone and try to secure an interview. There are over 700 daily and weekly newspapers throughout the country searching for news.

• **Magazines.** There are thousands of magazines catering to every market niche you can imagine. Offer reprints of a portion of your book in exchange for a free ad and-or a by-line at the end of your article. Do not neglect local and regional publications as they may be more accommodating to local authors. See *Magazines for Libraries* at the public library for a compete listing of magazines and their focus.

• **Television.** Wouldn't it be nice to have some of the major national talk show hosts invite you on their shows to discuss your book? That exposure could translate into an explosion of book sales. More realistic is being a guest on a local afternoon news program or a TV magazine talk show. Contact the show's producer with your story convincing him of a possible story angle for the show. TV leaves a memorable impression in the viewer's mind and can translate into short-term and long-term book sales.

Tip: If you are promoting your title through conventional channels of distribution, **inform** your wholesalers, distributor and bookstores of your promotional activities. This will insure they have your book on hand to fufill the demand you create, thus not losing sales.

❑ **Word of mouth Advertising.** The fastest and most efficient form of free publicity is word-of-mouth advertising. Anything you can do to get people talking about your book will help book sales. Publicity, promotion and favorable reviews all contribute to word of mouth advertising. The more books in people's hands, the better the chance they will spread the word. Success begets success.

❑ **Advertising.** Avoid paying for advertising until you have exhausted all forms of free publicity. Advertising comes in many forms, although the intent is always the same: to motivate people to buy. This is done by developing an ad that gains the reader's favorable attention, holds it long enough to get the intended message across and then motivates a desired response. When designing an ad, talk about the readers' interests, as they are interested in **gaining, saving, doing** or **being** something. Two general rules of advertising success are **timing** and **repetition.**

- **Space Advertising:** Space advertising involves placing an ad in books, newspapers, catalogs and magazines to reach your target audience. Orders are placed by the customer and received by you or your fulfillment service by mail or 800 telephone number and shipped via the mail. At the reference desk in the public library see:

Standard Rate and Data
Lists magazines, periodicals, demographics and their advertising rates.

Magazines for Libraries
Directory of national magazines by R.R. Bowker

Directory of Publications & Broadcast Media
Listing daily and weekly newspapers in the United States.

- **Classified Ads.** This is one of the least expensive forms of advertising. Classified ads are not used to sell something so much as to compile a good mailing list. The objective is to pull in inquiries about your book. A mailing list compiled from classified responses should yield high order levels. Offer free information in the ad by requesting a self-addressed, stamped envelope (SASE). Then send an article, flyer, brochure or any other promotional material. Code your ads to keep track of what works and what doesn't.

Tip: Before making a sizable investment in advertising, start small to test the effectiveness of your message. This way you can adjust your message until it yields the best results.

"Half the money I spend on advertising is a waste; the trouble is, I don't know which half."
John Wanamaker

• **Direct Mail Response Advertising.** If you can accurately identify your audience or niche, it is possible to sell books by direct mail from your home. Ask yourself: Am I prepared to handle the incoming mail response or should I use a fulfillment service? Is my product suitable to direct mail? Where can I advertise? Associations generally sell membership mailing lists or contact a mailing list manager. See *Encyclopedia of Associations* in the library for a listing of national associations.

Check into the legal regulations of mail order advertising in your state to follow the guidelines set forth by law. Write to the FTC and phone your State's Attorney General's office and request information about complying with those regulations:

Federal Trade Commission (FTC)
Pennsylvania Ave & 6th St NW
Washington DC 20580

Co-op mailing is combining your mailer with someone else's and then sharing the expenses. This reduces your mailing costs, but dilutes your message. Co-op with someone whose product is compatible with yours, to reduce competing or conflicting messages.

❑ **Mailing Lists.** Below are mailing list managers who specialize in renting or selling address labels and lists to book publishers. Request list types and pricing information.

Ad-Lib Publications
51-1/2 W Adams
Fairfield IA 52556
(800) 669-0773

American Booksellers Association
828 S Broadway
Tarrytown NY 10591
(800) 637-0037

Cahners Direct Mail Service
249 W 17th St
New York NY 10011
(800) 537-7930

Aggressive List Management
18-2 E Dundee Rd #101
Barrington IL 60010
(708) 304-4030

Para-Lists by Poynter
Box 2206
Santa Barbara CA 93140
(805) 968-7277

Twin Peaks Mailing Lists
Box 129
Vancouver WA 98666
(360) 694-2462

❏ **Author's Tours.** Do you like to travel? Does your book have a broad appeal? If so, author's tours can be a rewarding although expensive endurance test, but one of the best ways to reach a large book buying public. Pick the destination(s), and at least 6 weeks in advance, book yourself on as many TV and radio shows as possible. Inform all bookstores (in each area) of your promotional activity encouraging them to have your book in stock. Select the area's most popular bookstore in which to do a lecture or reading and booksigning. Send a notice to the local newspaper outlining your activity, as they may be interested in an interview or at least a mention in their paper. *Keep your wholesaler or distributor informed of your plans.*

Tip: Bring extra books in the event the bookstores
do not have your book in stock.

❏ **The Internet.** The Internet's World Wide Web is the most important new communication medium since TV and is a rapidly growing marketplace for selling books. Following are common ways to promote your book and services.

• Anyone can **offer help** in his area of expertise. Simply post an informative article and send to any discussion group *(newsgroup)* or bulletin board *(BBS)* catering to your market niche saying that you would be glad to answer people's questions about your subject of expertise. People who repond are potential customers for your book. Once you have established familiarity and trust, people will seek your advice. Be mindful of online etiquette when promoting your book. Check the FAQ's (frequently asked questions), which are usually posted within each discussion/newsgroup, for do's and don'ts.

- **Web Site / Home Page.** This is similar to having a store front on the Internet's World Wide Web that people can visit from their computer. It acts as an introduction to you, your book and your publishing venture with a collection of information capable of being presented in words, sounds, images and video clips. A Web site can include your on-going promotional programs, new book announcements, press releases, book reviews, author appearances, excerpts, a graphic of a book's cover, ordering information and even links to adjunctive services at other Web locations. When people visit your site, they may order, print or request additional information on your products or services. Check below and with your local *yellow pages* for online service providers about the cost and requirements to develop a web site.

Fortuity Publishing Services	Book Stacks Unlimited
Box 1025	200 Public Sq #26-4600
Woodacre CA 94973	Cleveland OH 44114
(415) 488-4260	(216) 861-0467
service@fortuity.com	info@books.com
http://www.fortuity.com	http://www.books.com

❑ **Discount Schedule and Policy.** Set a discount policy from the very start that is simple, clear and in writing so there is no misunderstanding. It is a requirement by the FTC that any discount you offer one dealer must be given to others who buy the same quantity. Your terms may differ when dealing with conventional channels of distribution as they typically work on a consignment basis only. Define your terms to include appropriate discounts to Wholesalers, Special Direct Sales (Alternative channels of distribution) and Bookstores. Include in your Terms and Conditions statement:

- Who pays the shipping and from where
- Breakdown of the quantity discount schedule
- Payment terms
- How to establish credit with you
- Return policy (if any)
- Special services such as *dropshipping & S.T.O.P.'s*

❏ **Shipping & Mailing Books.** When shipping pallets of books, use national trucking lines listed in the phone book. They base their rates on shipping location, weight, and freight class. Paperback books have a different and less expensive freight class than the standard book class rate (class 60 versus 65 respectively). UPS ground offers a fine service for smaller quantities and offers a pick-up service to contracted customers. Single copies can be mailed most economically through the Postal Service at **Book Rate,** or the lower **Library Rate** when mailing to Libraries. The Post Office also offers 2 lbs. **Priority** at a bargain price compared to the overnight express service, if an extra day or two delay won't make a difference. Shipping expenses add up quickly, thus it is good business practice to manage postage and shipping costs. If you are mailing large quantities on a daily basis, the phone book lists mailing services which specialize in sending bulk quantities.

A Final Note. Publishing and promoting your own book can be an enriching experience. At times things will not run smoothly, and you will ask yourself: *"What did I get myself into?"* Some discouragement can be expected. Meet other self-published authors in your area to pool resources and share experiences. This can be a source of encouragement, a way to shorten learning time and an opportunity to combine promotional efforts. Welcome to the world of publishing, and . . . **Good Luck!**

"Success comes to a writer, as a rule, so gradually that it is something of a shock to him to look back and realize the heights to which he has climbed."

P.G. Wodehouse

Subject Index

Index of Organizations and References

Self-Publishing Resources

❏ **A Simple Guide to Self-Publishing**
By Mark Ortman / 64 pages / $7.95

The place to start. This concise book is filled with time and money-saving tips to print, distribute and promote your own book.

❏ **The Self-Publishing Manual**
By Dan Poynter / 458 pages / $19.95

❏ **The Complete Guide to Self-Publishing**
By Tom & Marilyn Ross / 406 pages / $18.99

Both are very comprehensive books about self-publishing. Poynter's book is more thorough, but Ross's book is more readable. Each includes what you will need to write, publish, promote and sell your own book.

❏ **Book Publishing Resource Guide**
By Marie Kiefer / 378 pages / $34.95

An indispensable directory which includes the names, addresses, phone numbers and key contacts for thousands of book marketing channels and publicity outlets.

❏ **1001 Ways to Market Your Books**
By John Kremer / 544 pages / $19.95

Today's most complete handbook on book marketing featuring ideas, techniques, ways to plan promotions and sell your book.

❏ **Words That Sell**
By Richard Bayan / 127 pages / $13.95

A thesaurus of over 2500 words, phrases and slogans to help you write snappy promotional copy for your flyers, ads and brochures.

To order, send check or money order in US Funds to:

WISE OWL BOOKS
Box 621
Kirkland WA 98083

Shipping; $2.00 for the first book, $1.00 for each additional book.
WA State residents add **8.2%** Sales Tax

About The Author

Author, publisher and workshop leader Mark Ortman says; *"Getting my expectations bruised, and learning the hard way, have been my best teachers. Save yourself trouble by dreaming with your eyes wide open."* After receiving a Master's Degree in Communication from the University of Denver, he spent ten years working in the training and development field and he was the recipient of nine national instructional awards for his inspiring teaching style. His published work includes: *Now That Makes Sense!, So Many Ways to Say Thank You, The Teacher's Book of Wit,* and the award-winning *Simple Guide to Self-Publishing.* He also plays keyboards and has composed *Wednesday's Dream,* an album of instrumental music. Mark lives in the Seattle area.